# HORSES AND NEWPORT
## A Coaching Weekend
## 2018

### with Gloria Austin

## BROUGHT TO YOU BY

The books created by Equine Heritage Institute are designed to preserve the history and majesty of the horse. Our goal is to find, understand, and pass on the valuable data about equine use and its influence on humanity. The Equine Heritage Institute is a not for profit 503(c) and 100% of all proceeds from the sale of books, services, and products support Equine Heritage Institute's mission.

To make a donation to EHI, please visit www.ehi-donations.com

## SPECIAL THANKS TO

**Barbara Hess Auchter, Photographer**

Barbara Hess Auchter has been photographer and owner of Auchter Photography for over thirty years at www.AuchterPhotography.com. She enjoys capturing special events of all aspects of life. As an owner and breeder of Friesians, her personal passion is photographing horses. Barbara met Gloria Austin in Weirsdale, Florida because of Friesian horses and became enamored by the coaching world. Gloria's extensive collection of coaches, carriages, and horses developed in her an ongoing historical interest for the horse and carriage. Barbara has traveled the world photographing horses and coaching. Photographing the Newport Coaching Weekend of 2018 was an amazing opportunity to document a reenactment of an historical era of coaching. Barbara hopes you enjoy following Team Gloria Austin as they participate in this historic event.

**Brought To You By The Equine Heritage Institute**

# Gloria Austin's Collection of Books

## www.GloriaAustin.com

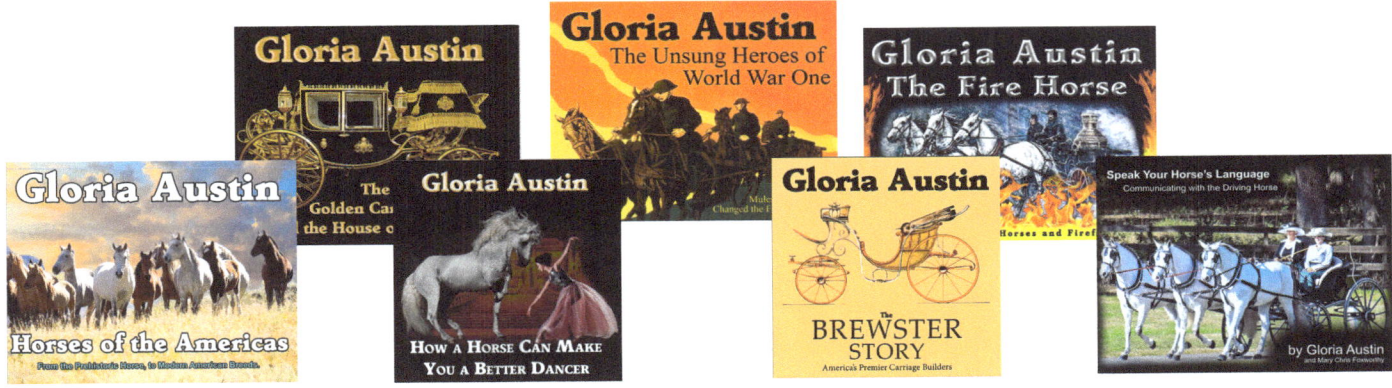

## ENJOY OUR OTHER BOOKS

- How a Horse Can Make You a Better Dancer
- The Brewster Story
- Carriage Lamps
- Gloria Austin's Carriage Collection
- A Glossary of Harness Parts
- Equine Elegance
- The Fire Horse
- Horse Basics 101

- The Unsung Heros of World War One
- The Horse, History, and Human Culture
- Horse Symbolism
- Horses of the Americas
- A Drive Through Time: Carriages, Horses, and History
- The Medieval Horse

- Speak Your Horse's Language
- Tea: Steeped in Tradition
- The Golden Carriage and the House of Hapsburg
- Women and Horses
- A Cookbook for Horse Lovers
- Dance! To Improve Riding and Driving

**Brought To You By The Equine Heritage Institute**

Horses and Newport
A Coaching Weekend - 2018
By: Gloria Austin - President of Equine Heritage Institute, Inc. (EHI)

First Publish Date May 2020
Copyright © 2020 by Equine Heritage Institute, Inc.

Cover photograph by Sarah Seaman

All rights reserved. No part of this publication may be reproduced, distributed, or transmitted in any form or by any means, including photocopying, recording, or other electronic or mechanical methods, without the prior written permission of the publisher, except in the case of brief quotations embodied in critical reviews and certain other noncommercial uses permitted by copyright law. For permission requests, write to the publisher, addressed "Attention: Permissions Coordinator," at the address below.

Gloria Austin Carriage Collection, LLC; Equine Heritage Institute, Inc.
3024 Marion County Road Weirsdale, FL 32195 Office: (352) 753-2826 Fax: (352) 753-6186

Ordering Information:
Quantity sales: Special discounts are available on quantity purchases by corporations, associations, and others. For details, contact the publisher at the address above.
Printed in the United States of America First Edition
ISBN: Print 978-1-951895-04-4, E-Book 978-1-951895-05-1

# Table of Contents

- 8     Foreward by Gloria Austin
- 10    Getting Ready for Newport
  - 11   Newport 2006 Staff
  - 12   Newport 2015 Staff
  - 13   Newport 2018 Staff
  - 14   Livery and Hats Galore
- 16    The Gilded Age of Coaching in a Weekend
- 18    THURSDAY
  - 20   Breakers and Chateau-sur-Mer Lawn Stabling
  - 45   Drive to Rosecliff and Miramar
  - 57   Drive to Hamilton Lunch
- 82    FRIDAY
  - 84   Morning Drive to Greenvale Vineyard Lunch
  - 104  Preparation for Miramar
  - 110  Drive to The Ledges
  - 119  Evening Drive to Miramar
  - 127  Miramar White Tie Dinner and Dance
- 142   SATURDAY
  - 144  The Elms Driving Exhibition
  - 166  Drive to Hammersmith Luncheon
  - 179  Breakers Ball Black Tie Dinner
- 194   SUNDAY
  - 196  Drive to Marble House Luncheon
- 210   Newport Locations

# The Horse

"We have had 6,000 years of history with the domesticated horse and only 100 years with the automobile."

*Gloria Austin*

# Forward  *by Gloria Austin*

Come along with me on an extraordinary trip to take a picture book look at a weekend few will ever get to experience.

What an honor it was to drive my English style coach and four beautiful grey Spanish horses at the most prestigious carriage driving event in the World – the Newport Coaching Weekend. This historic event unfolds amongst the grand Newport mansions as they provide a nostalgic backdrop for scenic drives on a horse-drawn turnout. I have been privileged to drive at this event three times and always enjoyed seeing the streets lined with spectators waiting to see the parade of carriages from a bygone era.

The Preservation Society of Newport County, with its Chief Executive Director Trudy Coxe leading the way, offers the New York Coaching Club and other specially invited guests an opportunity every three years to drive their elegant large 3,000-pound coaches on the streets of Newport, Rhode Island. The tradition of coaching originally came from historical England, where the Royal Mail was delivered by brightly dressed guards and brave drab-coated coachmen driving four horses on roadways in all types of weather. The respected skill of these drivers was replicated by wealthy persons in England. Eventually, the tradition came across the Atlantic to the United States. When the railroad and other forms of transportation replaced the horse, nostalgia prompted the development of coaching as a sport to be enjoyed by those with the skill and resources.

Aprons or lap robes cover the legs of the driver and all passengers. These were used to protect the fine clothing of the guests on board. Road dust and flying horsehair was not attractive on one's clothing when stopped for lunch or dinner. These lap coverings were left on the coach for use on the return trip. Rain gear is also carried on the front interior seat in the event of the occasional storm. The coach carries a stick basket for walking sticks and umbrellas. When intended for protection from the sun, these appointments are called parasols and are essential. Sometimes a horn is carried in a leather or wicker basket attached to the rear seat, as well.

The horn sounders sits on the rear Gamon Seat and stands when tootling on a natural horn – one with no valves. The five to seven notes are achieved with changes in the armature. The sounders play Coach Horn Calls and Coach Horn Tunes. Calls can include: Get Ready, The Start, Clear the Road, Slacken Pace, Pull Up, Higher Up, Off Side, Near Side, Change Horses, Steady, and Home. Tunes might include Lambs to Sell, Fun On The Road, Oh Dear What Can The Matter Be, Old Times Chorus, and Buy a Broom. Coach Horn Tunes can also be created for special coach drivers who have achieved some degree of status. I am proud to say the Canadian Tootlers wrote a tune for me called "Twig, Tweet, and Trot," for my love of nature, the out-of-doors, and horses.

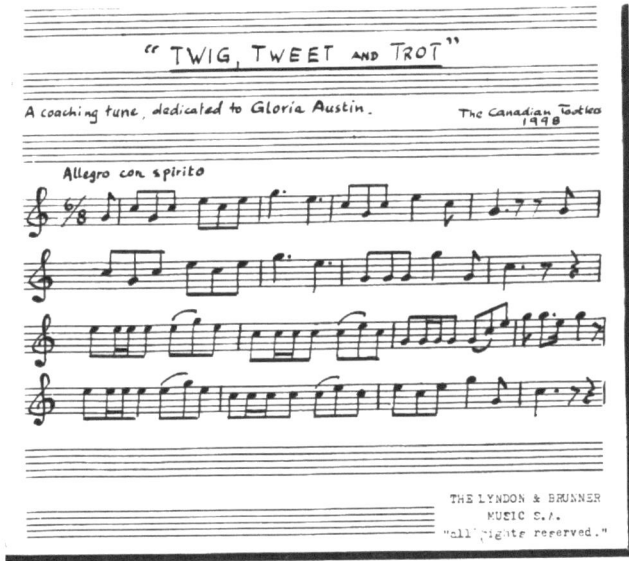

The driver uses the reins, voice, and whip to signal the horses to start, stop, turn, and stand. This skill is called Four-in-hand Driving – meaning four reins held in the left hand and manipulated by the right hand and rotations of the hands and wrists. Even though not perceivable, we use our entire bodies when driving – our arms, bodies, and legs. We sit on a wedge seat, so we drive in a semi-standing position. We try to make it look easy, but this system was developed by English coachmen who drove great distances as well as through the narrow streets of London, Paris, Philadelphia, or New York. The skill development requires time and sensitivity to the training of horses.

Women and men both wore hats appropriate for the season and weather conditions. Women's styles of hats have changed over the ages, but usually, the larger the carriage, the larger the hat! Evenings still required a hat, but men wore black top hats in the evening, and women wore brimless hats or fascinators as there was no sun on their faces.

Parties are essential! Eating with friends is a social activity valued by all. It is also a dress-up time when the fine outfits are worn for the opportunity to be seen and dance after dinner and dessert.

The camaraderie and sharing many beautiful experiences of this Newport Coaching Weekend prompted the preparation of this book. As a woman, I am doubly honored to participate. Enjoy this book and the Preservation Society of Newport County's next Coaching Weekend.

# Getting Ready for Newport

A carriage driver carries a whip to signal to the horses, and is thus called a Whip. Getting an invitation is an honor particularly if you are not a member of the New York Coaching Club, whose members are all competent "Whips." As a driver, I must be competent with four horses to a coach. I also must have properly trained horses and a skilled and trained staff.

The organizer of the daily drives, Frederick (Ted) Ayers, requires that each driver have a proper coachman or coachwoman capable of driving the horses from our lunch or dinner venues back to the stable. Melissa Warner (2006), David Saunders (2015), and Robert Longstaff (2018) have each served in this capacity. In 2018, Mindy, Emily and Scott Spurgeon, a family of horse people played various vital roles in the orchestrated event. Emily and Mindy acted as grooms caring for the horses and harness. Scott sounded the horn and was responsible for preparing the coach each day.

Conditioning the horse to go 10-12 miles with proper shoes for travel on the Newport asphalt roads requires planning and preparation weeks and months in advance. Trucks and trailers must be prepared for the trip and all the clothing and harness and extra bits and pieces must be loaded. I put two trucks each with a trailer on the road. One, the special horse trailer, takes the horses, their food and supplies. The other, a cargo trailer, takes the coach, harness and clothing for the event. The trip itself requires planning for fuel and overnight stops from Weirsdale, Florida to Newport, Rhode Island. The drivers of the trucks must have special licenses and training to drive rigs that measure as much as 65 feet. In 2018, we did have a truck break down within the last few miles of Newport, but Frederick Ayers and Lynn and Raymond Tuckwiller saved the day. Frederick loaned the Tuckwillers his truck to pick up our trailer that carried the coach, so we did not miss any of the organized drives.

---

**Gloria Austin's Newport Staff**

Grooms at Newport in 2006
Michelle Dlugoborski
Kacy Tipton-Fashik
Nanette Elliot
Melissa Warner, private coachwoman
Dale Rominoli, horn sounder

Grooms at Newport in 2015
Michelle Dlugoborski
Emily Spurgeon
David Saunders, private coachman
Ray Tuckwiller, horn sounder

Grooms at Newport in 2018
Emily Spurgeon
Mindy Spurgeon
Vaughn MacDonald, stable prep
Robert Longstaff, private coachman
Scott Spurgeon, horn sounder

# Newport 2006 Staff

Gloria Austin and Melissa Warner

Kacy Tipton-Fashik and Michelle Dlugoborski

Dale Rominoli, horn sounder

Exhibition at The Elms

# Newport 2015 Staff

Gloria Austin's 2015 Newport Staff and Friends

Gloria Austin, David Saunders, and Ray Tuckwiller

Michelle Dlugoborski

Gloria Austin and Dr. Gene Serra

Ray Tuckwiller

Emily Spurgeon

## Newport 2018 Staff

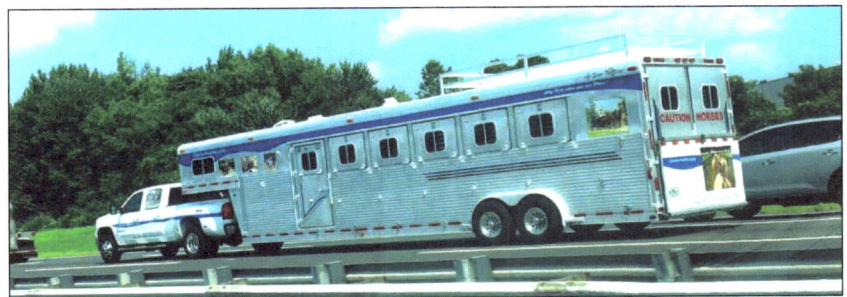
Driving from Weirsdale, FL to Newport, RI

Gloria Austin and Robert Longstaff

Vaughn MacDonald

Gloria Austin and Dr. Gene Serra

2018 Newport Staff and Friends

Scott Spurgeon

Gloria Austin and Robert Longstaff

Mindy Spurgeon

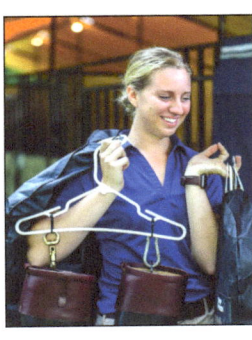
Emily Spurgeon

*Newport Coaching Weekend*

## *Livery and Hats Galore*

Now of course, the clothing and hats are important! Livery outfits must be cleaned and checked, shirts and breeches must be looking their best, and hats must be fitted and cleaned. Scott, a sounder who is new to blowing the horn, had to practice and learn all the calls and a few basic tunes including my custom composed "Twig, Tweet, and Trot." I had to lay out each day's outfits for myself and my partner Dr. Gene Serra since we were to attend each day's social luncheon and dinner. Gene's and my hats had to also be organized to go with each outfit. I prefer to wear light colored hats and outfits, so I am noticed. I also drive light colored horse for the same reason.

For special occasions, such as Newport, I prepare yellow rose corsages for my grooms and myself. The yellow rose is the flower of the World Coaching Club, the women counterpart to the New York and British Coaching Clubs. Robert Longstaff, my coachman for this outing, wore the blue cornflower of the men's organization.

I also wore at my neck the symbol of a four-in-hand driver – silver lead bars. These are miniatures of the large bar. There are three, one main bar and two side bars that are positioned at the rear of the two front horses. These bars are used when the leaders are needed as extra horsepower, to pull on the end of the pole between the two wheel horses. As a woman driver, I have a reputation of wearing pearls when I drive so I prepared necklaces, bracelets and pearls of each day.

Invitatiion to Wednesday night Whips Dinner

*Newport Coaching Weekend*

# The Gilded Age of Coaching in a Weekend

Attendees were transported back to the 19th century as authentic horse-drawn coaches paraded through the streets of Newport and the grounds of the Newport Mansions on Thursday, August 16 - Sunday, August 19, 2018 for the triennial renewal of a Weekend of Coaching, hosted by The Preservation Society of Newport County.

SPECIAL EVENTS

DRIVING EXHIBITION
On Saturday, August 18, The Elms hosted a driving exhibition on the back lawn. Spectators got an up-close look at each of the teams while learning the history of each coach as their whips guide them around the back lawn.

COACHING DINNER DANCE
The weekend culminated with a formal Black Tie Coaching Dinner Dance at The Breakers on Saturday evening.

PARADE ROUTES
Each day from Thursday through Sunday, the visiting whips drove their coaches on a different route through Newport as they traveled to private social events, much as their 19th century predecessors did on a daily basis.

Thursday, August 16 Morning Drive to Price's Neck (with Breakers and Rosecliff drive thru)

Friday, August 17 Morning Drive to Greenvale Vineyard

Friday, August 17 Evening Drive to Miramar (limited coach participation; 3-4 teams)

Saturday, August 18 Drive to Hammersmith (after Elms Exhibition)

Sunday, August 19 Morning Drive to Marble House (with Breakers drive-thru)

THE TRADITION OF COACHING

The New York Coaching Club was formed in the latter part of the 19th century, eventually becoming part of the social fabric of Newport in the summer. The Wetmore's, the Bells, the Vanderbilts, and the Belmonts were all active members, bringing their coaches together to go to the races, the polo games, and the Casino.

The two types of open-air vehicles used in the sport of coaching—a Road Coach and the slightly smaller Park Drag—employ a team of four horses. All seating is outside, with the driver, known as a "whip," sitting in the slightly elevated right front seat, and a relative or coachman taking up the "box seat" on the left. The rear bench of the coach holds at least two specialized footmen called grooms. Two center benches can hold up to 10 passengers.

The "whips" who were expected to attend: Mr. S. Tucker S. Johnson, of Hobe Sound, Florida, President of the Coaching Club; Ms. Gloria Austin, of Weirsdale, Florida; Dr. Timothy J. Butterfield, of Derry, New Hampshire; Mr. Frederick E. Eayrs, Jr., of Middleboro, Massachusetts; Mr. Walter F. Eayrs, of Mapleville, Rhode Island; Mr. William G. Ginns, of Skeffington, Leicester, United Kingdom; Mr. James Granito, of Southern Pines, North Carolina; Mr. John Frazier Hunt, of Spring City, Pennsylvania; Mr. Herbert Kohler, of Kohler, Wisconsin; Mr. Charles T. Matheson of Middleburg, Virginia; Mr. James Mather Miller and Mrs. Misdee Miller, of Lakewood Ranch, Florida; Sir Paul Nicholson, of Durham, United Kingdom; Mr. Louis G. Piancone, of Gladstone, New Jersey; Mr. Harvey W. Waller, of Stockbridge, Massachusetts; Mr. Glenn Werry, Jr. of Edwards, Illinois; Mr. George A. Weymouth, of Chadds Ford, Pennsylvania; and Mr. John White, of Newton, New Jersey.

# THURSDAY

**August 16, 2018**

❶ 10:00 am Breakers Stables Departs
   10:30 am All Depart from Chateau-sur-Mer
❷ 11:00 am Rosecliff Drive thru and Miramar Stop (Invite Only)
   12:00 pm Little Stop (Invite Only)
   12:30 pm Brenton Point
❸ 12:45 pm Hamilton Family Luncheon

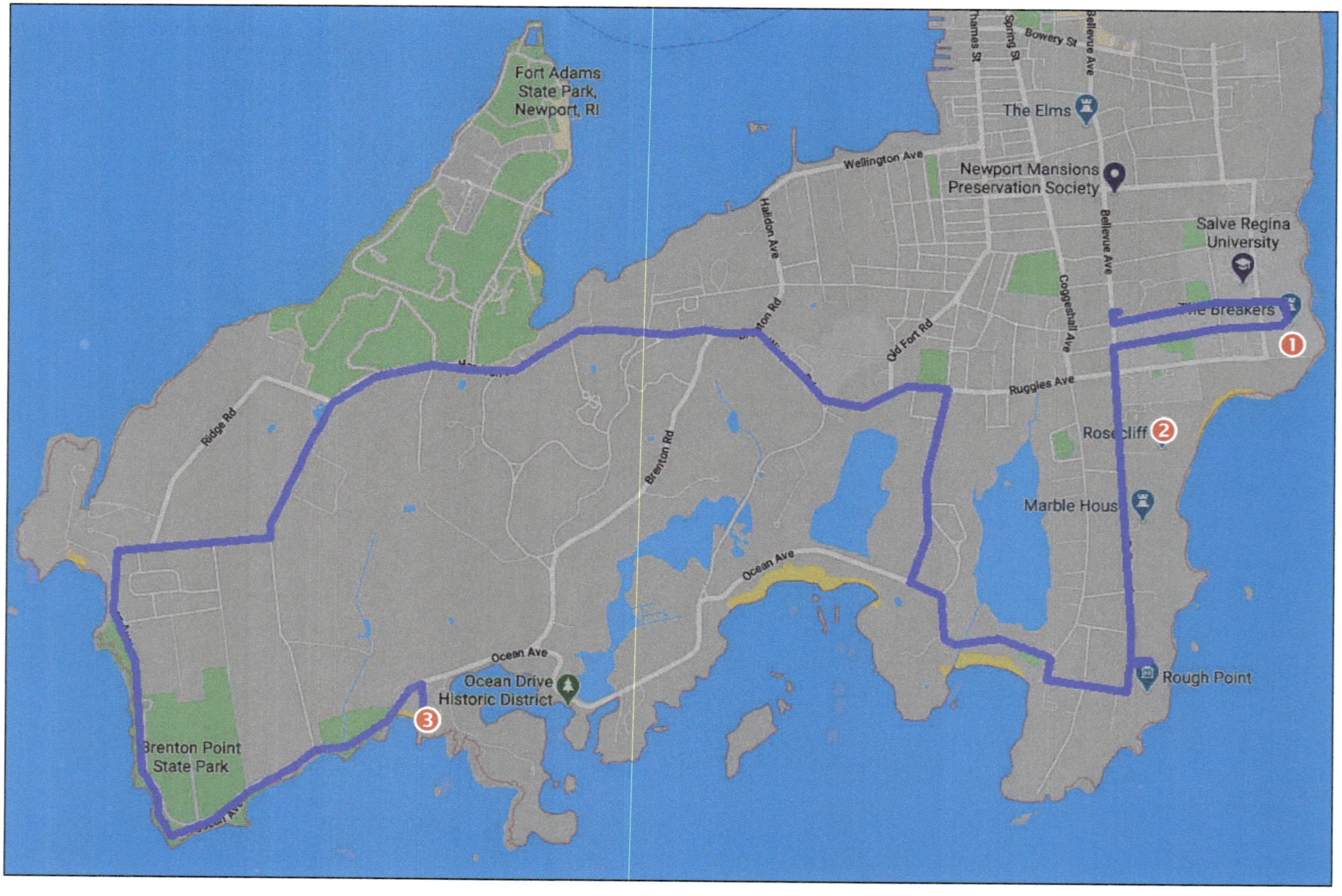

### ❶ Breakers and Chateau-sur-Mer Lawn Stabling pg 20

After hours of travel from Weirsdale, Florida to Newport, RI, everyone is happy to arrive at the site of the stables set up and waiting for the four horses called The Austin Grays. The lush treed lawn at the Breakers and Chateau-sur-Mer gave us a place to greet friends from the United States and from Europe.

*A Nod To The Past:* "The dream was Paul Downing's - an idea born four years ago as he stood in the silent Breakers Stable and Carriage House wishing it were alive again with horses, grooms, and well-turned-out carriages.

... The Breakers Stable has become a museum displaying some of the Vanderbilt carriages and harness, but not since the original owner's grandson, Governor William Vanderbilt, sold the last of the Coaching teams, had there been hay, straw, and horses in the handsome red brick building.

Spotless white stable coats, new brass pillar chains on the stall heel-posts, friendly greetings called down the line of stalls among grooms - overnight, the atmosphere of a museum was charged with the excitement and activity of a working carriage stable." (cited. The Carriage Journal, Vol 6. No 2. Autumn 1968. The Newport Conference of The Carriage Association of America, Inc.)

### ❷ Drive to Rosecliff and Miramar pg 45

The grand homes of Rosecliff and Miramar made for beautiful stops in the August heat. My gray Spanish horses appreciated a rest after trotting on the hot Newport pavement. Our passengers enjoyed icy drinks and light treats while we were greeted by our host and hostess.

### ❸ Hamilton Lunch at Sea Edge pg 57

The first luncheon of the weekend. Hosted at the 14 room mansion summer home of Campbell Soup heiress Dorrance "Dodo" Hamilton. Hamilton had bought the house in the 1990s and restored it. The estate had been built in 1902 for Albert H. Olmsted, the brother of famed landscape architect Frederick Law Olmsted, the designer of New York City's Central Park.

*Newport Coaching Weekend*

# Breakers Chateau Lawn Stabling

*Newport Coaching Weekend*

*Some of my greatest joys are reuniting with old friends and meeting new ones. The conversation is always lively.*

*The setting at The Breakers and the excitement of our first day at Newport is stimulating and fun. European friends who belong to the Private Driving Club are enthusiastically welcomed.*

*Newport Coaching Weekend*

*There is always news to share even though we all follow one another on social media.*

*Newport Coaching Weekend*

Newport Coaching Weekend

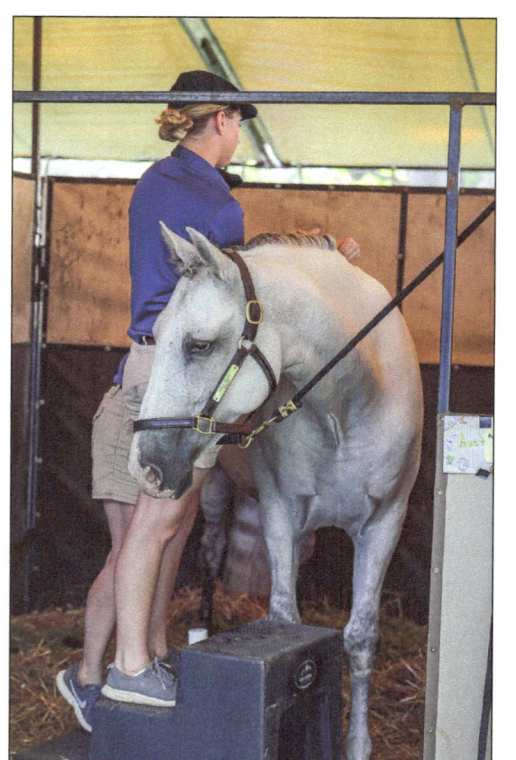

*Coaching Meets, as these occasions are called, are quite a production. We must organize the people, the horses, the coach, and the appointments at the correct place for the correct time.*

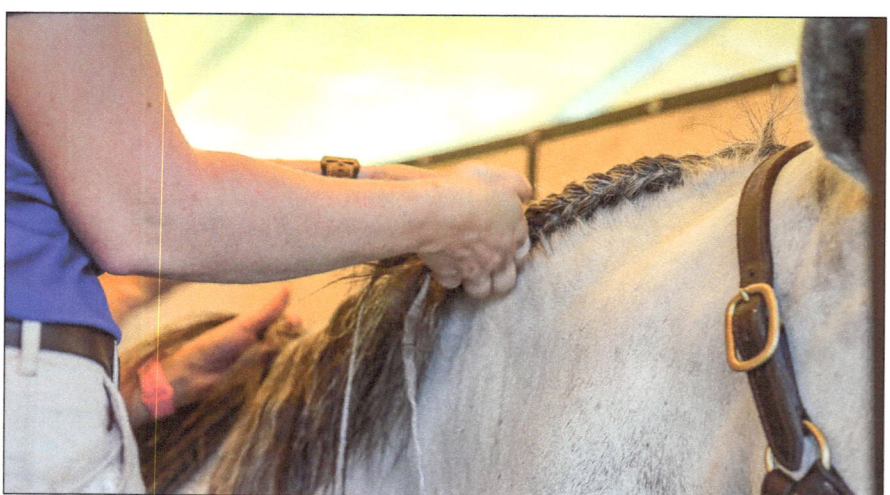

*Newport Coaching Weekend*

Newport Coaching Weekend

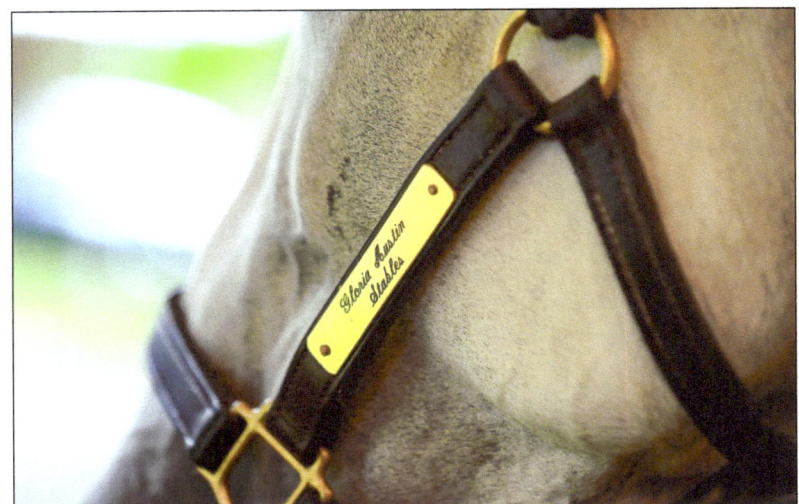

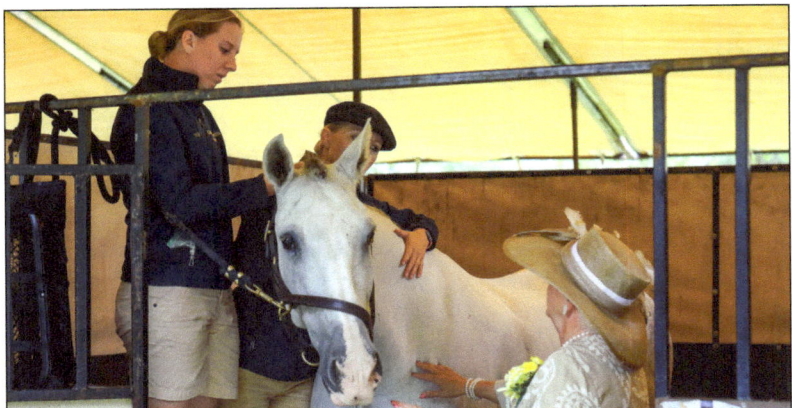
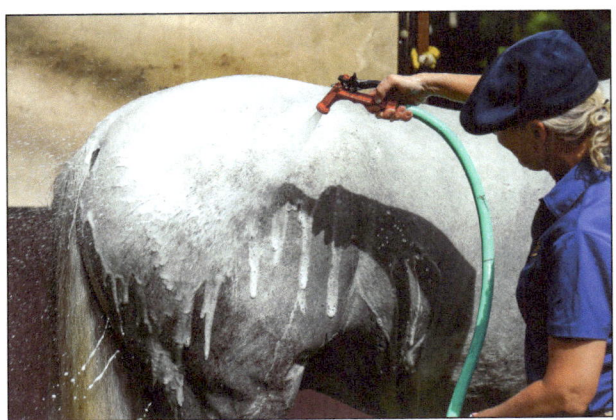

*Newport Coaching Weekend*

*I always wear pearls and my necklace with "lead bars." These are the bars to which the two lead horses are attached to aid in pulling the coach.*

*Newport Coaching Weekend*

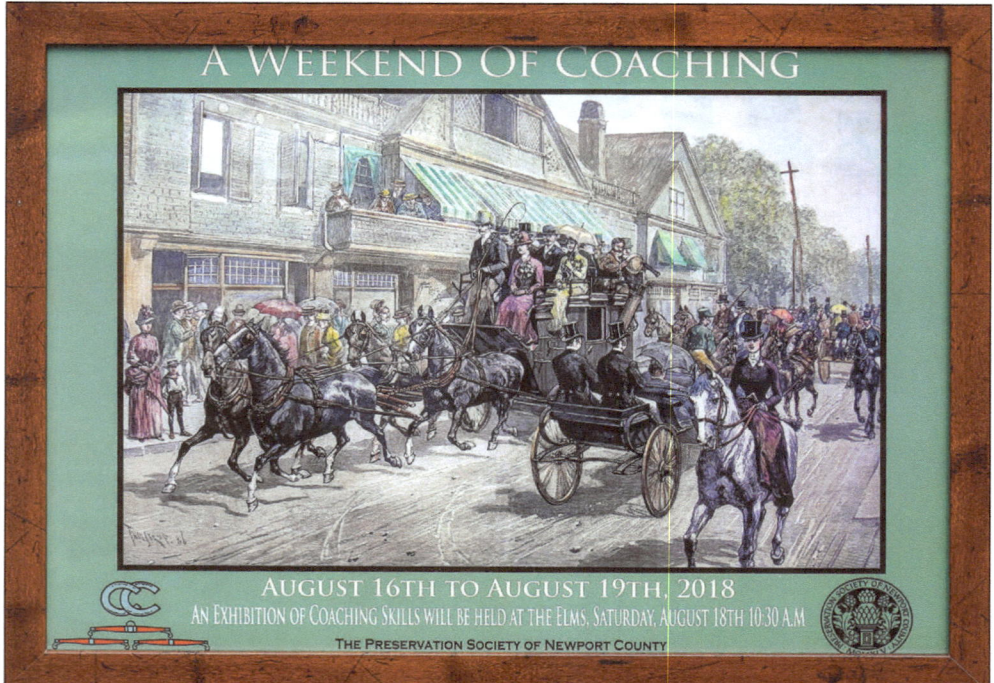

The Preservation Society of Newport County produces a poster as a memento of the occasion. They are treasured memories.

You will notice the horses and the young beautiful children steal the show.

Newport Coaching Weekend

*Newport Coaching Weekend* ............................ 33

*Newport Coaching Weekend*

*The process of "putting to" is a sight to behold. The horses are brought out two-by-two, and I am handed the reins. I wear the Yellow Rose of the World Coaching Club, the all women's organization. The horses and attendants all don their boutonnieres.*

*Newport Coaching Weekend*

*My private coachman makes sure the harness and attachments are all correct and then puts on his apron to protect his clothing from the road dust and loose hair of the horses. He stays close at my left side to take over the reins when I get down from the box seat.*

*Newport Coaching Weekend*

> *Guests mount the carriage. Many who ride with us are horse enthusiasts and eager to experience an opportunity few have.*

Newport Coaching Weekend · · · · · · · · · · · · · · · · · · · · · · · · · · · · · 37

*Newport Coaching Weekend*

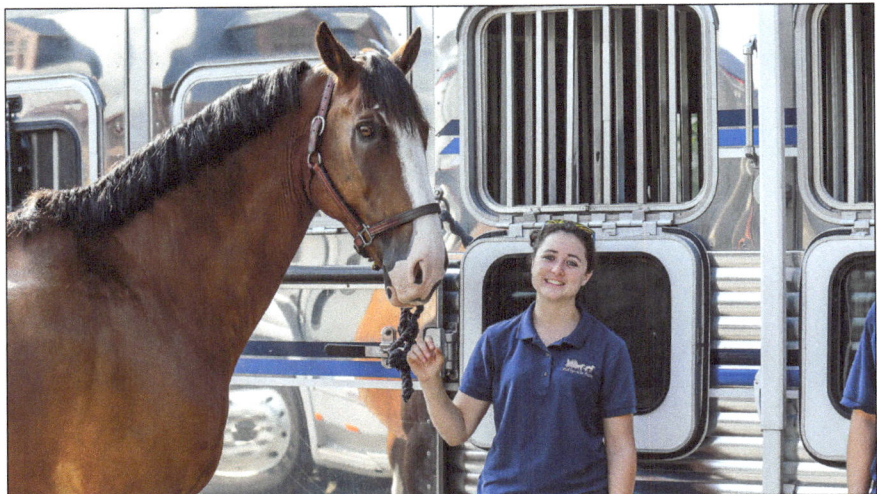

*It is difficult for most to understand the work involved in this event, not only for the organizers, but for those putting on this living show.*

*Newport Coaching Weekend*

*Newport Coaching Weekend*

*Newport Coaching Weekend*

*Newport Coaching Weekend*

*Our "order of go" is dictated by seniority. This means there is a wait for others to proceed in front of my turnout. Fortunately, my horses are well trained to wait patiently and follow other coaches.*

*Newport Coaching Weekend*

*Newport Coaching Weekend*

# Drive to Rosecliff and Miramar

*Newport Coaching Weekend*

> *You can see the perspiration on the horses' darkened gray coats. Like humans, horses are one of the few mammals who sweat through their skin.*

*Newport Coaching Weekend*

*Newport Coaching Weekend*

*You can tell how well we are treated at each rest stop. And you also know how useful a parasol is in the hot sun.*

Newport Coaching Weekend

*Newport Coaching Weekend*

*Newport Coaching Weekend*

*Newport Coaching Weekend*

*Newport Coaching Weekend*

Newport Coaching Weekend

# Drive to Hamilton Lunch

*Newport Coaching Weekend*

*Newport Coaching Weekend*

*On extremely hot days, The Coaching Club, will suspend its rule that gentlemen must wear jackets. This day was such a day. Shirt sleeves were acceptable, but gentlemen and ladies always wear hats when on a carriage.*

*Newport Coaching Weekend* ............................................................ 61

*Newport Coaching Weekend*

*Newport Coaching Weekend*

*Newport Coaching Weekend*

*Newport Coaching Weekend*

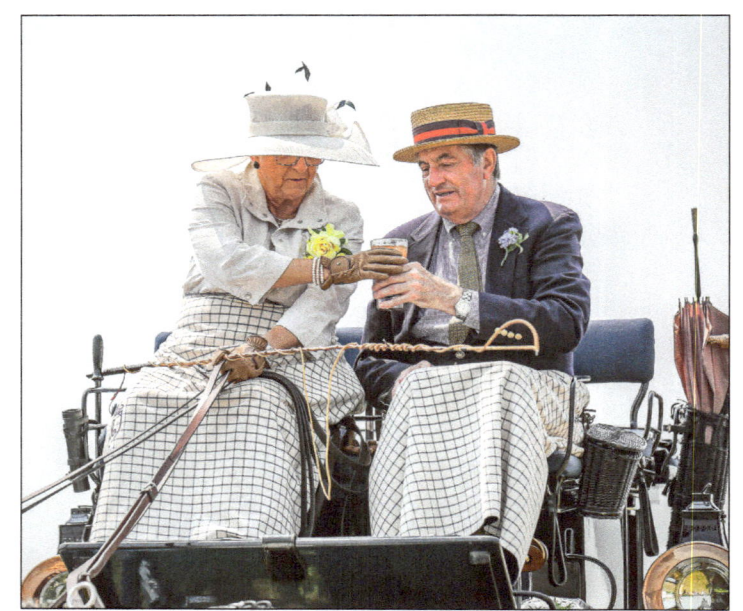

*Newport Coaching Weekend*

*Newport Coaching Weekend*

*Ascending the hill on the lawn of the Hamilton House after a long drive requires I "spring the team" which means to canter all four horse up the hill to get momentum to make the climb. The road gait of the carriage horse is the "trot" since it is the most sustainable gait over a long distance.*

*Newport Coaching Weekend*

*Newport Coaching Weekend*

*The arrival at each stop, holds its rewards for man and horse alike. It is now that everyone is willing to stand quietly.*

*Newport Coaching Weekend*

*The size of the homes at Newport are beyond description. The open-air views abound in this beautiful setting where we replicate the use of these great horses that have served mankind for millennia.*

Newport Coaching Weekend

Newport Coaching Weekend

*Newport Coaching Weekend*

*Newport Coaching Weekend*

*Newport Coaching Weekend*

*Newport Coaching Weekend*

*The respite gives us another chance to meet even more luncheon guests who are eager to socialize with enthusiastic coach drivers.*

*Newport Coaching Weekend*

*The luncheon setting under large tents offer plenty of space to gather and eat scrumptious delicacies.*

*Newport Coaching Weekend*

*Newport Coaching Weekend*

*Newport Coaching Weekend*

# FRIDAY

**August 17, 2018**
   10:00 am Depart Breakers
   10:15 am Depart Chateau-sur-Mer
   11:10 am Clambake
❶ 12:45 pm Vineyard

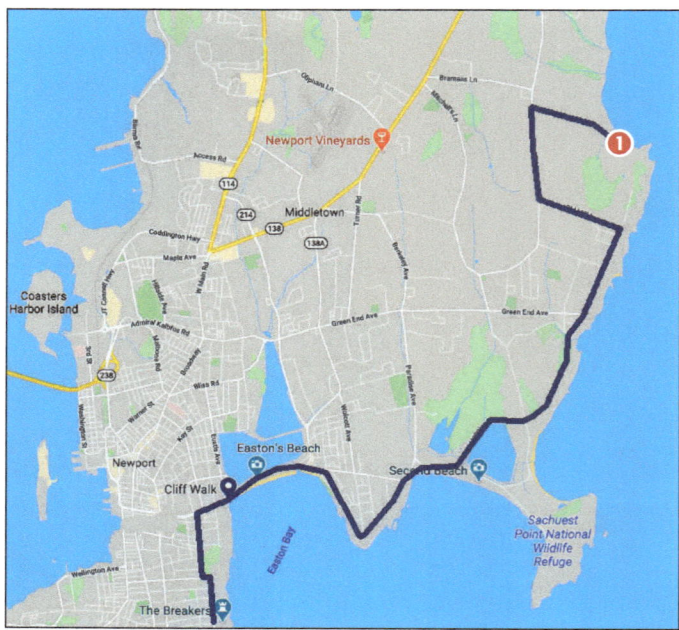

❶ **Morning Drive to Greenvale Vineyard Luncheon pg 84**

Since I was honored to drive in the evening to Miramar, I did not drive the horses to the Greenvale Vineyard Luncheon. Gene and I traveled there by car. At the luncheon, a woman tripped over a tent stake and Gene used his medical skills to assess her condition, so she could contiune to enjoy the event with her friends.

*A Nod To The Past*: "The Friday afternoon Driving Marathon, first public appearance of the carriages, ... With Mr. Talbot calling out the order of departure, the 12 carriages started along the Marathon route promptly at 3 p.m. Thousands of spectators waited eagerly along the roads. Children hung from trees, others followed on bicycles; elderly ladies peered out from cars parked along the route, and as the carriages neared Bailey's Beach, young people in bathing suits raced to the road to cheer and call out, "Man, that's real cool.!"

A brief lineup for picture taking ... ended the afternoon's drive. After refreshments were served to all association members as well as the whips and their passengers ..., it was time to depart for the Association's official conference banquet back at the Viking Hotel. (cited. The Carriage Journal , Vol 6. No 2. Autumn 1968. The Newport Conference of The Carriage Association of America, Inc.)

**August 17, 2018**
    5:00 pm Depart Breakers
    5:15 pm Depart Chateau-sur-Mer
    5:40 pm Newport CC (Private)
    6:15 pm Brenton Point
❶ 6:45 pm The Ledges (Private)
❷ 7:35 pm Miramar (Private)

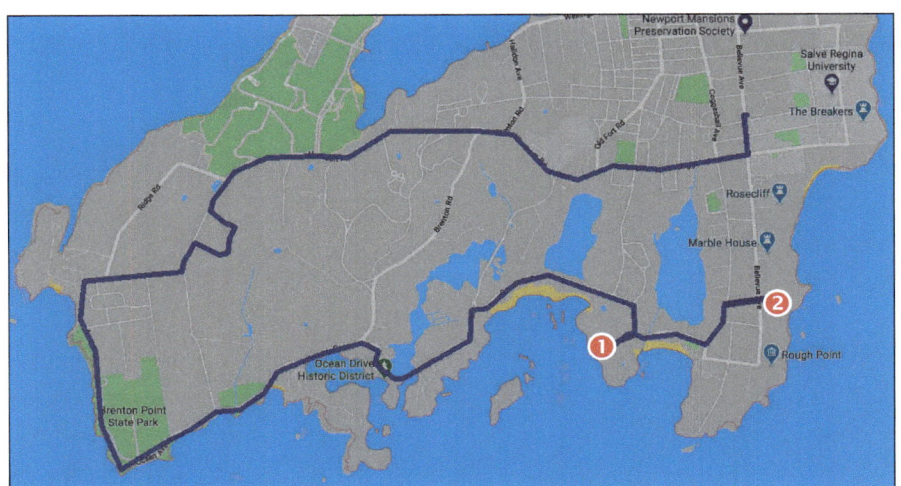

❶ **The Ledges pg 110**

The staging of the drive to Miramar required we stop at The Ledges, a beautiful Victorian home. This gave us all an opportunity to light the lamps attached to the sides of our coaches. It is spectacular for onlookers to witness the carriages with the sparkle of lighted candles that can be seen from miles away.

❷ **Miramar White Tie Dinner and Dance pg 127**

This private home was newly refurbished and became a spectacle with the lights of the night. I have attended some great parties in castles in Europe, but this rivaled all others. A huge tent had to be erected to accommodate the invited Whips, their guests, and guests of the host and hostess at this gala dinner and dancing evening.

*Newport Coaching Weekend*

# Morning Drive to Greenvale Vineyards Lunch

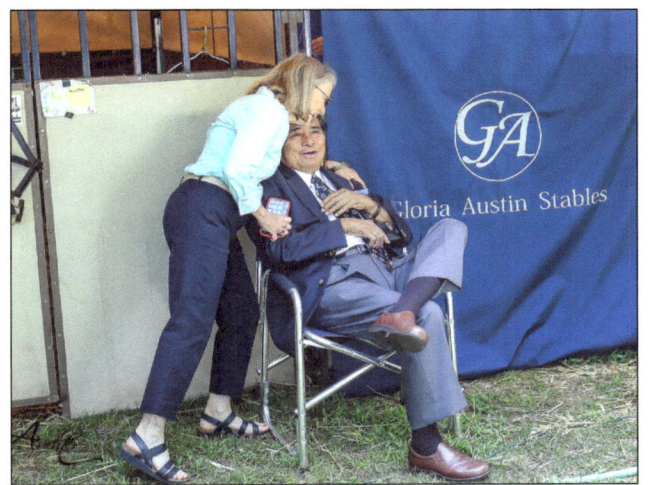
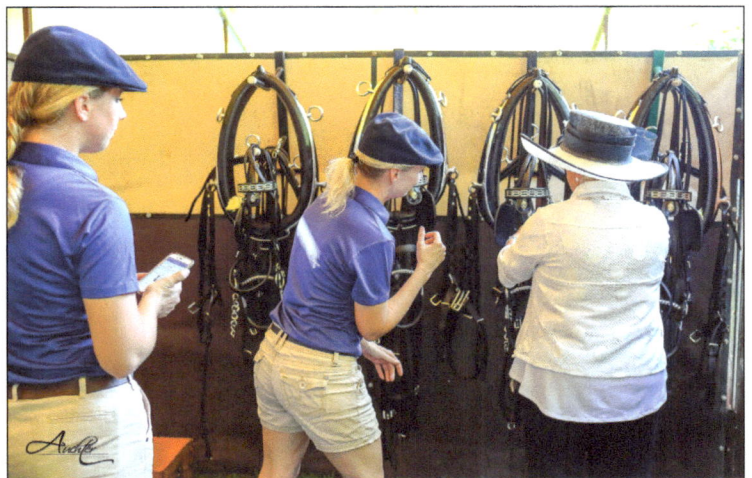

*We always take time to photograph the workers who turn this affair into a sight to behold. Everybody knows their job so we can all be relaxed as we do our individual tasks.*

*Newport Coaching Weekend*

*Newport Coaching Weekend*

*Newport Coaching Weekend*

*Newport Coaching Weekend*

*It was fun to just be a spectator of the drive to Greenvale Vineyards. Its tasting room and breathtaking landscape offer great venues for private tours, weddings, and special events.*

*Newport Coaching Weekend*

*You can see what a responsibility it is to drive four horse to a 3,000-pound coach full of friends and relatives.*

*Newport Coaching Weekend*

Newport Coaching Weekend

*Newport Coaching Weekend*

*Newport Coaching Weekend*

*The children are brought in tow. They also are sharing the moments that will create lasting memories.*

Newport Coaching Weekend

*The Greenvale Vineyard staff had plenty of wine for all to enjoy.*

*Newport Coaching Weekend*

*Newport Coaching Weekend*

*Newport Coaching Weekend*

*Newport Coaching Weekend*

*Newport Coaching Weekend*

*Newport Coaching Weekend*

*Newport Coaching Weekend*

*Newport Coaching Weekend*

# Preparation for Miramar

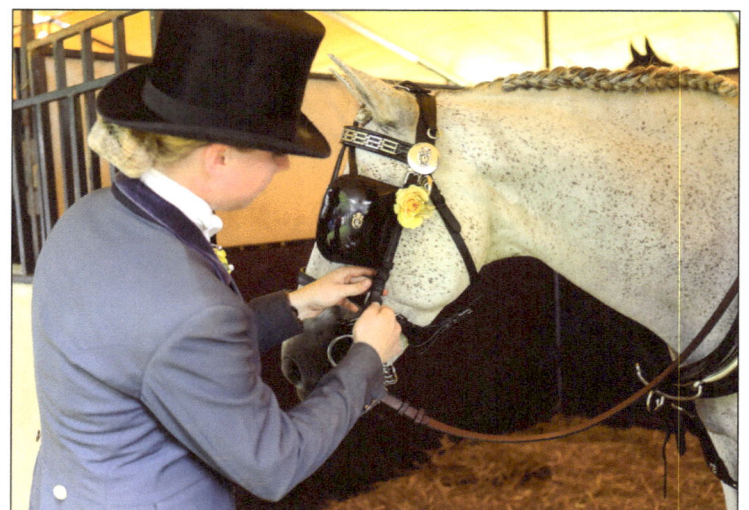

*It is white tie, and tails and a yellow rose for the gala ball at Miramar. Horses and people must be readied.*

*Newport Coaching Weekend*

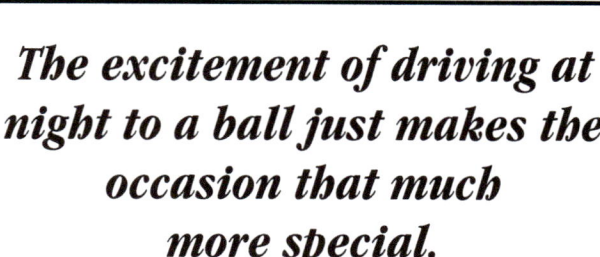

*The excitement of driving at night to a ball just makes the occasion that much more special.*

*Newport Coaching Weekend*

*Our procedure of "putting to" is well routinized, so no mistakes are made.*

*Newport Coaching Weekend*

*After the wheelers are put to, the leaders are brought in front and attached to the lead bars.*

Newport Coaching Weekend

*All must be attentive and alert.*

*Newport Coaching Weekend*

# Drive to The Ledges

*Newport Coaching Weekend* ·········· 111

112 · · · · · · · · · · · · · · · · · · · · · · · · · · · · · · · · · · · · *Newport Coaching Weekend*

*Newport Coaching Weekend* · · · · · · · · · · · · · · · · · · · · · · · · · · · · · · · · · · · · · · · · · · · · 113

*Newport Coaching Weekend*

*Newport Coaching Weekend*

*Newport Coaching Weekend*

*There is always a last-minute trip to the powder room before we make our grand entrance at Miramar with splendidly clad guests awaiting our arrival.*

*Newport Coaching Weekend*

*Newport Coaching Weekend*

# *Evening Drive to Miramar*

*Newport Coaching Weekend*

Newport Coaching Weekend

*Newport Coaching Weekend*

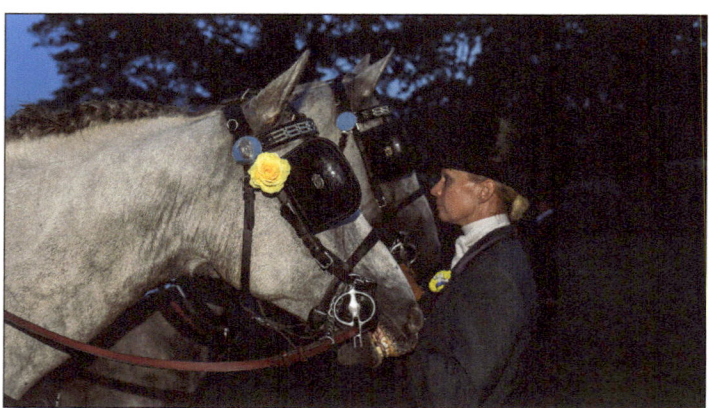

*Newport Coaching Weekend*

*There is always the famous group picture of all those skilled Whips - coach drivers who carry a whip. Americans and Europeans alike, the horses all drive the same, whether in England, France, or the USA.*

Newport Coaching Weekend

> *The hosts and guests are always in their best and ready to be seen. There are handsome men and beautiful women, all at the same party.*

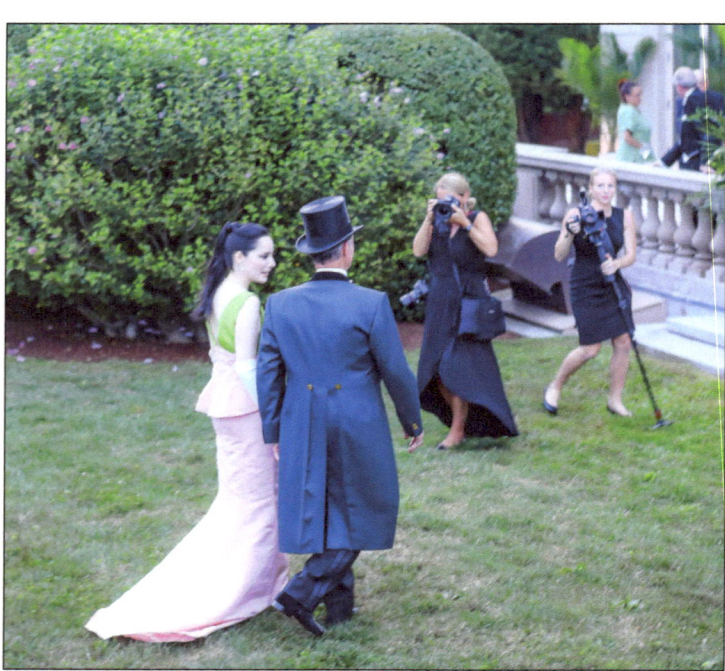

This is where the private coachwomen or coachmen come in handy. They are the skilled drivers that take the horses and coaches back to the stable while Gene and I and the others attend the party.

Newport Coaching Weekend

*After the Whips and their guests are dropped off for the Ball, we ride back with the Coachman or Coachwoman for our own party, usually held at the Breakers stables.*
*-Michelle Dlugoborski, Groom*

# Miramar White Tie Dinner and Dance

Newport Coaching Weekend

Newport Coaching Weekend

*Newport Coaching Weekend*

*Newport Coaching Weekend*

*Newport Coaching Weekend*

*Those who host the parties and lead the coaching organizations put in alot of work. Each of the drivers were honored with an introduction, The occasion - dinner, fireworks, and the dancing - was spectacular.*

*Newport Coaching Weekend*

*Newport Coaching Weekend*

Newport Coaching Weekend

*Newport Coaching Weekend*

*Newport Coaching Weekend*

*Newport Coaching Weekend*

*Newport Coaching Weekend*

# SATURDAY

**August 18, 2018**

❶ 11:30 am Leave Elms
    11:45 am Past Harbour Court
    12:15 pm Brenton Point
❷ 12:45 pm Hammersmith Farm (Private)
❸  6:00 pm Breakers Ball Black Tie Dinner

*A Nod To The Past*: "The Discovery that the Navy Band would lead the parade of carriages through the streets and into the Park caused a rush to be last in line among the members who were driving. Mrs. Hayden politely turned down Mr. Talbot's offer to lead off just behind the band. Finally Mr. Ferguson volunteered, and his well-mannered Morgans went at a controlled trot behind the blaring horns." (cited. The Carriage Journal , Vol 6. No 2. Autumn 1968. The Newport Conference of The Carriage Association of America, Inc.)

### ❶ The Elms Driving Exhibition pg 144

The presentation of the coaches at The Elms is **the** triennial event. Thousand of people observe the beauty of a promenade of coaches on the lawn.

*A Nod To The Past:* "The driving program, brilliantly narrated for the Association by past president Sidney Latham, included harnessing demonstrations, precision driving, repeated turns around the oval by each vehicle and a steady stream of driving lore and Texas humor which kept the audience of some 2,000 in their seats applauding for more. From Mr. Latham the uninitiated learned the differences between a Park Drag and a Road Coach, a tandem and a random, a unicorn and a spike, the "near" and the "off" side. The obvious enjoyment of the whips seemed contagious. When the horn blowing competition came at the end of the program, the audience cheered each tune, melodious or tortured. Mrs. Robinson drew the final cheer for versatility and good sportsmanship when she handed the reins to her husband, stood up on the box of their Coach, and sounded a rousing cavalry 'charge" on their Coach horn." (cited. The Carriage Journal, Vol 6. No 2. Autumn 1968. The Newport Conference of The Carriage Association of America, Inc.)

### ❷ Drive to Hammersmith Luncheon pg 166

*A Nod To The Past*: "The ... first public appearance of the carriages, started at Hammersmith Farm. Luncheon tables set on the terrace of the great mansion overlooked a pasture sloping down to the sea where the 12 different vehicles assembled. The "Venture" was there with Mr. and Mrs. Seabrook on the box and Mrs. Barbara Brewster Taylor, daughter of famed carriage builder William Brewster, among the passengers." (cited. The Carriage Journal , Vol 6. No 2. Autumn 1968. The Newport Conference of The Carriage Association of America, Inc.)

### ❸ Breakers Ball Black Tie Dinner pg 179

Over 500 friends and supporters of the Preservation Society attended the ball at the Breakers manison, a palatial reproduction of a 16th century Italian villa that took two years and $5,000,000 to complete in 1895.

# The Elms Driving Exhibition

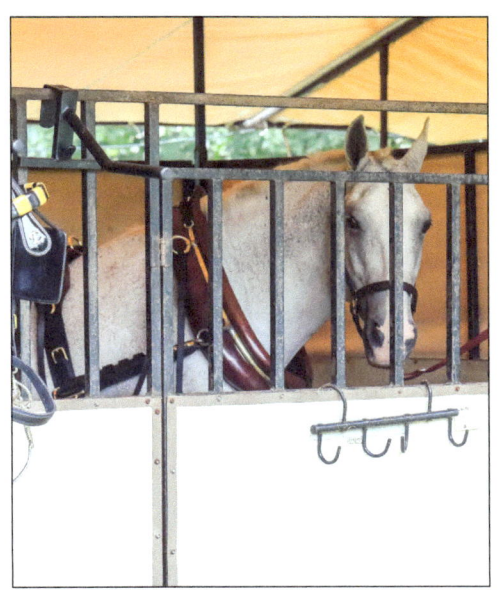

*Newport Coaching Weekend*

*This day is special with a promenade and stop in front of a large crowd at the mansion called The Elms. Honored guests are assigned to each coach to sit atop a Gamon seat.*

*Newport Coaching Weekend*

*The brightly colored commercial Road Coach carries a spare collar and special tools in case of a breakdown on a long road trip.*

*Newport Coaching Weekend*

*Most passengers are joyfully perched high in the air. The Whips or drivers must be attentive to their tasks every moment.*

*Newport Coaching Weekend*

*Newport Coaching Weekend*

*Newport Coaching Weekend*

*You will notice coaching horses come in all colors, but the four in each team (as four are called) are generally of matching color.*

*Newport Coaching Weekend*

> *The coaches also are painted a variety of colors. The Park Drags are solid color whereas the road coaches are brighter and have lettering on their bodies. The names on the sides of the Road Coach are of the towns and taverns where they stopped.*

*Newport Coaching Weekend*

*The carriage at the top is called a break or a dog cart. A break, because its driver's seat (box seat) has a toe board and a seat on risers like the Coach. This carriage is called a Dog Cart because of the louvers in the body. These louvers allowed air to pass into the hunting dogs container, often built under the seats.*

*Newport Coaching Weekend*

Newport Coaching Weekend

*Newport Coaching Weekend*

*Newport Coaching Weekend*

*Newport Coaching Weekend*

Newport Coaching Weekend

*Newport Coaching Weekend* · · · · · · · · · · · · · · · · · · · · · · · · · · · 161

*Newport Coaching Weekend*

*Newport Coaching Weekend*

*Newport Coaching Weekend*

*Newport Coaching Weekend*

# Drive to Hammersmith Luncheon

*Newport Coaching Weekend*

*Newport Coaching Weekend*

*Newport Coaching Weekend*

*Newport Coaching Weekend*

*Newport Coaching Weekend*

*Newport Coaching Weekend*

*Newport Coaching Weekend* · · · · · · · · · · · · · · · · · · · · · · · · · · · 173

*Newport Coaching Weekend*

*Newport Coaching Weekend*

*Newport Coaching Weekend*

*Newport Coaching Weekend*

*Newport Coaching Weekend*

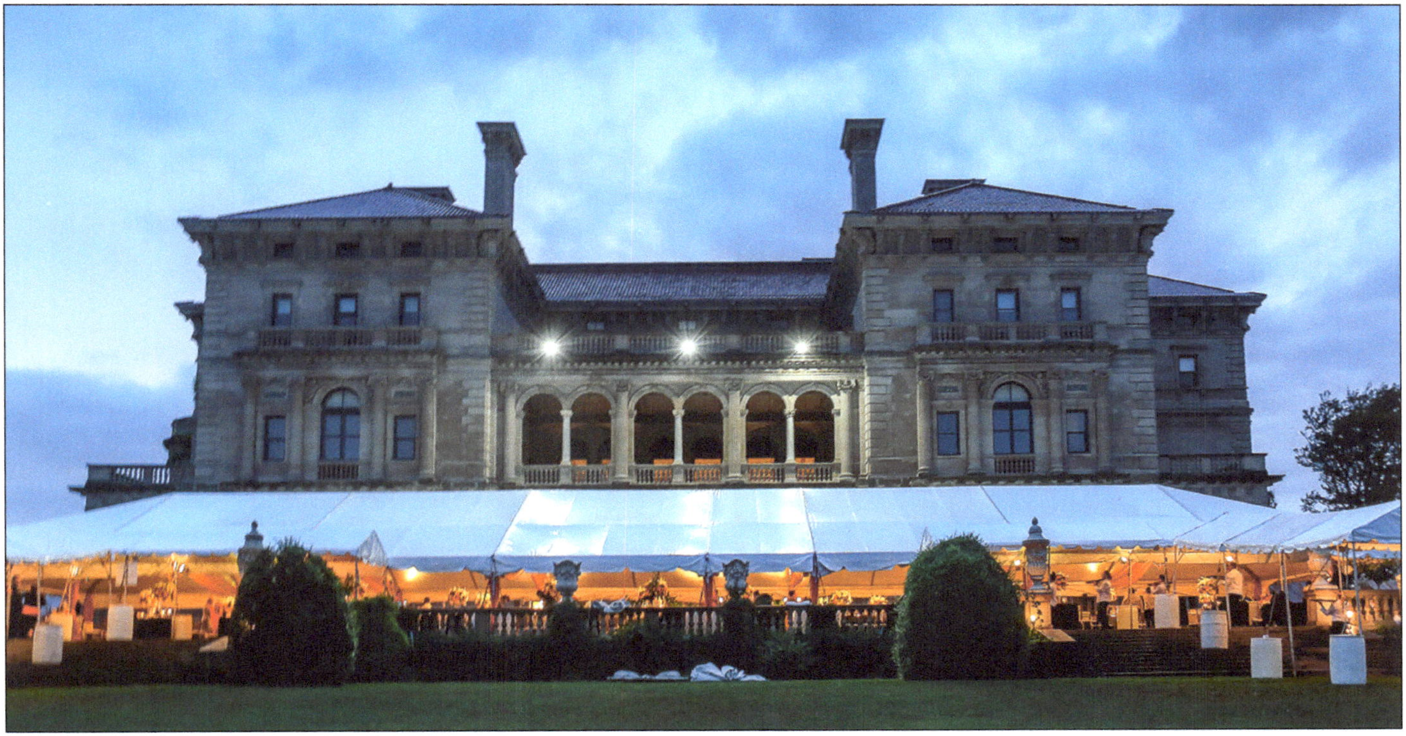

# The Breakers Ball Black Tie Dinner

Newport Coaching Weekend